EVERLASTING SPRING

-when a loved one dies

EVERLASTING SPRING

-when a loved one dies

Philip W Williams

ILLUSTRATED BY
AUDREY TEEPLE & KEITH RAINER

FALCON

A FALCON BOOK

published by
Church Pastoral Aid Society
Falcon Court, 32 Fleet Street, London, EC4Y 1DB

distributed overseas by
Australia: Emu Book Agencies Ltd, 63 Berry Street, Granville, NSW 2142
Canada: The Book Society of Canada, PO Box 200, Agincourt, Ontario
New Zealand: Scripture Union Wholesale, PO Box 760, Wellington
Singapore State: SU Christian Book Centre, 36H Prinsep Street, Singapore
South Africa: SUBASA, 83 Camp Ground Road, Rondebosch 7700, Cape Town

EVERLASTING SPRING

THE AUTHOR DEDICATES THIS BOOK TO NANCY, JASON AND JENNA

ISBN 0 85491 545 1
Originally published in the United States as 'When a Loved One Dies' (Augsburg) 1976
First published in the United Kingdom as 'Everlasting Spring' (CPAS) 1977

DESIGNED AND PRODUCED IN THE UNITED KINGDOM
photoset in Baskerville type and bound by
Richard Clay (The Chaucer Press) Ltd, Bungay, Suffolk
printed offset litho by
Fletcher & Son Ltd, Norwich

Preface

'Blessed are those who mourn, for they shall be comforted' (Matthew 5:4). This is good news to any of us who has been deprived, robbed of a life, who has lost a loved one. Jesus, our Lord, with intuitive sensitivity towards people, encouraged grief and bereavement. He was saying, 'Do it! Grieve!' Why? He knew its potential for good. He knew we would eventually receive blessing and comfort. Jesus saw no virtue in being tough-as-nails, brave, unfeeling, stoical when experiencing the loss of a loved one. Experiencing the loss, having and showing feelings, re-examining attitudes and beliefs – all are necessary and Christian. To grieve and go through bereavement is to move from hurt to health. If we do not go through bereavement, bitterness, sickness, and even death may result.

Jesus knew that grief and bereavement were normal and necessary. He also knew that when we give ourselves permission to do this work – and it is work – we shall receive God's blessing. We shall be able to affirm life once again.

There is no typical grieving person. Each of us is only typical of what is particular and peculiar to himself. There are many common grief reactions, but we each experience the loss of a loved one in our own way.

This book is not meant to be a book of what you, as a grieving person, *should* be experiencing. This book doesn't describe the right and only way to grieve successfully. Many sections will ring true for you: 'That's how I feel. That's me. That's where I am.' Some sections will seem unrelated, inapplicable, perhaps far-fetched. Other sections may hit too close and be rejected.

But you are you and this is your book. Make this book yours in whatever way it applies to you. You don't need to start at the beginning. Read whatever section seems to strike your present need, feeling, or curiosity.

God bless you in your bereavement journey – not a journey without pain, but an adventurous journey that can be, in time, graciously good.

Contents

page

5 **Preface**

9 **It can't be true**

12 **I don't believe it**

15 **If only**

18 **I could cry**

21 **I'm so angry**

25 **Going down**

29 **I'm not feeling well**

32 **I can't go on**

36 **Here, but gone**

39 **Here and nowhere**

43 **Lord, not my child!**

46 **You'll never know**

49 **I know**

53 **A swinging pendulum**

56 **Much ado**

59 **Yes**

62 **Through a glass darkly**
65 **There is a season**
69 **Those old feelings**
71 **Reaching and touching**
76 **Constant care**
79 **Springs in the desert**
83 **The prized possession**
86 **A mustard seed**
88 **The community of faith**
91 **What lies beyond?**
94 **Amazing grace**

It can't be true

A mother and father walked down the hospital corridor from the emergency ward to a waiting room, filled with fearful anticipation. Wrinkles of tense pain showed on their faces. All they could hear was the sound of their own shoes on the marble hallway.

In the waiting room the dreaded news came, straight and simple. 'We did all we could to save her. I'm sorry, but your daughter has died.'

The mother began to shake. Screams, tears, agony poured out. 'No, no, it can't be true. Not my little girl!' The father sat silently, rigid. Slowly tears came, forcing their way out of eyes that had just seen a truth they couldn't believe. Shock set in. 'It just can't be true.'

News of the death of a loved one may create within us a temporary numbness or state of anesthesia. This is an eerie unreal feeling, but it is natural, necessary, and helpful. Shock is a built-in buffer that helps us tolerate the crunching news or fearful scenes of death.

God has built into us this natural buffer for the initial blow. It is a good gift because it

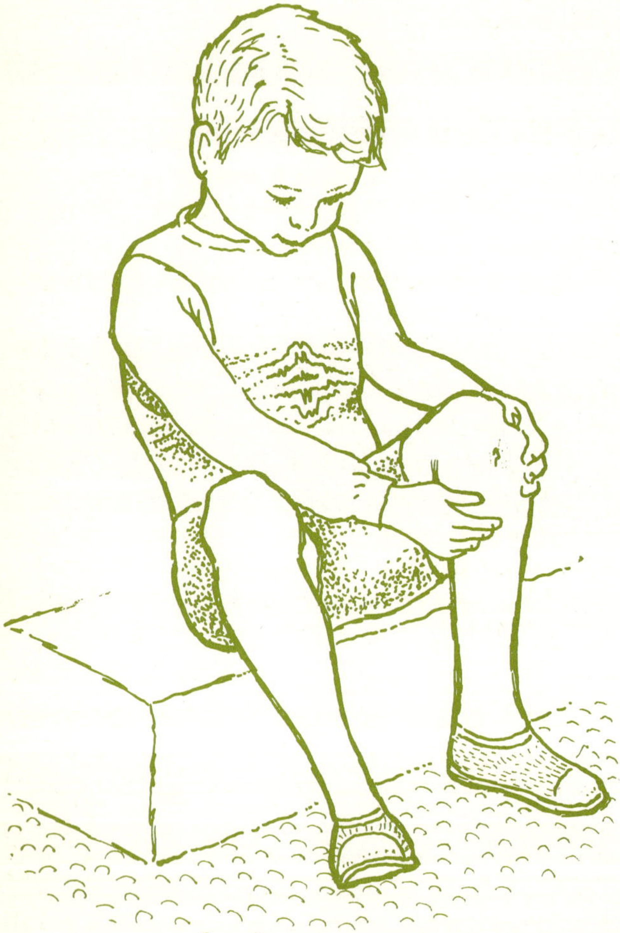

protects us. There is no way for any of us to comprehend totally the initial loss of a loved person. Shock numbs us and gives us time to get ready for our bereavement journey. We need it, yet only for a time. Then we must move on. Yet, as we move into our bereavement journey, it is common to revert to the time of shock. One husband said, 'My wife died two years ago, but I still have moments when it seems that she really hasn't died.' These flashes occur, but they don't stay.

God has given us a good gift in shock. It is a clue that we are in the beginning of our journey. We may feel we can't go on, or that we never will want to go on, but it is good to know that we have been protected in the midst of an overwhelming, painful loss.

Scripture reading

Psalm 77:1–10; John 11:17–36

Dear Father, I hurt and I need protection. Help me to understand that shock is a sign of your built-in protection to help me weather the eye of the storm. As the storm slowly fades, help me to leave the shock and to move forward in my bereavement and in my life. Amen.

I don't believe it

After the headlines, comic strips, letters to the editor, and sports, many people turn to the obituary column of a newspaper. The language used in an obituary announcement is revealing: 'Mr Edward Praif passed away December 3.' 'Mrs Lucille Agner was promoted to glory last evening.' 'Wanda Sue Smith was taken Wednesday evening.' We know death is real, yet our language often reveals our difficulty in accepting the reality of death. *Death* and *die* are practically obscene words to some people. It's as if saying those words will make the death of a loved one too real.

Denial is natural. If we see something that offends our sight, we close our eyes. If something stinks, we hold our nose. If something is ugly, we try to make it look pretty and pleasing. When we lose a loved one through death, we may normally and naturally deny our deep loss for a time. Yet, if this denial continues and we suppress the reality of this death, we may become ill and need help.

I have often heard people remark how well

someone took the death of a loved one. The bereaved appeared controlled, having everything in hand, perhaps managing to be a superb host or hostess during the early bereavement process. This may be helpful to some people, but usually it means someone is struggling hard to deny the death: 'I don't believe it' or 'I *won't* believe it.'

But we need not be cool heroes when a loved one dies.

We are human beings created by a God who knows the heart of life and of man. We are created by a God who knows that denial can fortify hope and prevent despair – for a time. But prolonged, total denial can only lead to a despair that sees no hope, no triumph.

Recall the number of times Jesus attempted to prepare his disciples for his death. They wouldn't hear of it. They denied it. Few people want to hear the words of impending death, yet Jesus urged them to be prepared and to move through denial to acceptance and hope.

I still recall the words of a twelve-year-old daughter to her parents, who had steadfastly denied her impending death: 'Don't worry, I'm going to die today, but it's OK. I'm going to be with Jesus.' These words showed her own acceptance, and they could have helped her parents move from 'I won't believe it' to 'I do believe it.'

Scripture reading

Psalm 4; Psalm 31; Matthew 7:7–8; Luke 18:35–42

Dear God, I find it hard to accept things I don't want to be true. How can I bear up in the face of my loss? If I face my loss, I might lose control. I might have to feel pain rather than feeling nothing. Help me not to fight so hard to deny the death of my loved one. Help me to move in my journey with you. I trust you. I know you will not leave me. Amen.

If only

'Do you think if we had left sooner for the hospital it would have made a difference?'

'She never would tell us when she had those pains, but I could tell. If only I had insisted and dragged her to the doctor sooner.'

'I shouldn't have let him go out tonight. I had a feeling . . .'

'What if we had gone to one of the big London hospitals instead of here? They have more specialists. Maybe they could have done something.'

'There was more to talk about, if only we had had more time.'

There is always some guilt when any of us loses a loved one. This isn't unusual. None of us can live close to another person and love deeply without hurting that person. We do and say things we later regret. We know they hurt our loved one.

Intimacy, closeness, is built by loving and hurting and reconciling. We can't really learn to love unless we are willing to run the risks of hurting and failing. Losing someone we love reminds us of those hurts and failings, of words we regret saying, incidents we'd like to forget, actions we'd like to take back. We feel guilty.

Or we may be that person who has stayed faithfully in the waiting room of an intensive care unit hour after hour, day after day. Then we leave the ill person as fatigue, home responsibilities, and family needs set in, or as the loved one seems to regain strength. What happens if this loved person suddenly takes a turn for the worse and dies? We blame ourselves for not having been there.

If we were to continue in this *if only* guilt, we would be unrealistically assuming that our presence would have made the difference in our loved one's living or dying. We would be assuming an unreal power and control over life and death; a power and control we simply do not possess. An analyst said to Robert Anderson, 'You are experiencing a guilt that denies what we are, which is, of course, a human being – fallible, needful, of limited saintliness.'

It hurts deeply not to have been there. We feel guilt since we wanted to be there. But if this guilt is prolonged, we may need some professional help in working through it.

When we feel we are beginning to accept ourselves, guilt's hold is broken. One grieving person said, 'I began to realize there was more I could do. As I let go of my guilt, I felt more at ease with myself. I began to like myself. I experienced the assurance of forgiveness which the pastor pronounces each week in the worship service.'

God has provided some beautiful resources to help us in our guilt. Church worship contains public or private confession and absolution. The Scriptures proclaim an accepting Lord who continually forgives people. This same Lord and Saviour died for us in an ultimate act of forgiveness, and he rose to give us new life. He has given us the Lord's Supper to strengthen us and to reconcile us with God.

Guilt is real. The Bible shows us our guilt, but it also reveals a gracious God who forgives us. A college professor once said something that speaks to many life crises, certainly to the guilt of if only. He said, 'The greatest prayer anyone can pray is, "Create in me a clean heart, O God, and renew a right spirit within me." '

Scripture reading
Psalm 25; Luke 7:36–50

Dear God, I get so entangled with my doubts, my regrets, my wrongs. I even plague myself with my guilt. Get through to me, Lord! I need to know that there is forgiveness and acceptance with you. I need to accept myself. Remind me of the cross, the greatest sign of your forgiveness. Amen.

I could cry

Mrs Brown had lost her husband after a sudden heart attack.

'You look as if you could cry.'

'I won't.'

'Why not?'

'I prefer to be alone. When I get started I can't stop. I'll let it out when I'm finally home.'

But she didn't cry, even at home.

A man had just seen his ten-year-old daughter die. He checked back tears. Relatives encouraged him to hold on, to be brave. 'Don't cry!' Rather than expressing the hurt of his loss, he pleased the relatives as long as he could.

The friends and relatives said, 'Weren't they remarkably strong and poised. They really went through the funeral well. You have to admire them.' But do we?

What is wrong with tears? The idea that big boys or big girls don't cry is a mistaken assumption. Not to cry, ever, is unnatural and borders on being inhuman.

Many of us have been led to believe that crying is not good. In men it is thought unmanly, a sign of weakness. But we forget that, when he lost his good friend, Lazarus, Jesus wept. We may have learned this as the shortest verse in the Bible. We many not have learned its basic human message: 'Cry! It's good. It's human. It's Christian.'

Nine-year-old Tommy had lost his grandfather. During the funeral vigil, Tommy and an old friend, Mr Walters, talked together. Tommy asked, 'Mr Walters, do you ever cry?'

The old man answered, 'Yes I do. I cried when your grandfather died, for grandpa was my friend too.'

Tommy said, 'I didn't cry! Why did you cry?'

'I cry when I'm hurt,' Mr Walters replied. 'I was deeply hurt by grandpa's death. It was a hard loss. He was such a good friend to me and even more to you.'

Eventually Tommy cried too.

Tears don't erase all the hurt. Tears don't bring the dead to life. But tears do help to ease the pain.

In their book *Up from Grief*, Bernadine Kries and Alice Pattie tell about a young widow who was told by everyone not to cry in front of her six-year-old daughter. They said it would leave emotional scars. She took their advice, and it proved to be bad. One day her daughter asked, 'Why didn't you love daddy? You were glad he died!'

This young widow then realized what she had done by not crying in front of her daughter. They then cried together, and things were easier for both of them.

When Jesus drew near to Jerusalem shortly before his own death, he saw the city and he wept over it. Jesus cried over a city and its people! How much more we need to show our hurt when death claims a loved one.

Scripture reading

Psalm 42:1–4; Ecclesiastes 3:1–4; 2 Corinthians 1:3–5

Dear God, Jesus points the way for me to be honest with my feelings. Sometimes I fear embarrassment or misunderstanding. Sometimes I fear being pitied or put down. Sometimes I fear the intensity of my own hurt. Help me to understand and express what I feel. If you understand, I can too. Amen.

I'm so angry

What happens when a person I love dies? Dare I be angry? Is it wrong for a Christian to be angry?

When friends lost a child in an automobile accident I was angry and questioned, 'God, why? Why?' Job's wife was even more direct. When her children died, she angrily shouted at Job, 'Curse God and die!'

We are God's people, humans with feelings. This includes a capacity for experiencing the emotion of anger. If we lose a person or thing close to us, we react. Any relationship of worth is filled with rich, personal investment. We don't want to lose this. When we do, we may well feel anger. We may feel it like an erupting inner volcano or it may be a slow burn. We may feel a general irritability or a lingering bitterness. Some bereaved people have used words such as the following to describe anger: 'I could flare up at anytime'; 'Stupid little things upset me'; 'My nerves are on edge'; 'I feel a turmoil inside.'

To feel angry is natural, normal. To be angry is a potential part of the healing process. This is a part of being a bereaved Christian. To suppress anger and never let it out can lead to a deeper than normal depression.

We may be angry at God. It is hard to accept that life is unsure and that death is an uncertain certainty. These thoughts make us feel powerless. Being angry is a natural, desperate attempt by us to control the order of things, since God seems to have let us down.

The anger may be at people around us. I vividly recall the death of my favourite dog, Brownie, when I was a young boy. He was hit by a jeep and left at the road's edge. Walking beside my father, I pulled the little wagon which carried my dog. I felt anger well up. I lashed out at the neighbours who drove that jeep and killed my friend. To me, he wasn't a dog, he was a person! If a dog is a person to a child, what about a loved one who really is a person?

The anger may be at those who cared for our loved ones – doctors, nurses, attendants, relatives. It certainly may be directed at people who press us toward accepting our loss too soon, before we've worked through our feelings and thoughts.

We may even be angry at our loved ones. As one lady very honestly admitted, 'I'm so angry at Joe for dying first! He always took care of the finances. I never did any of that. Now I have to,

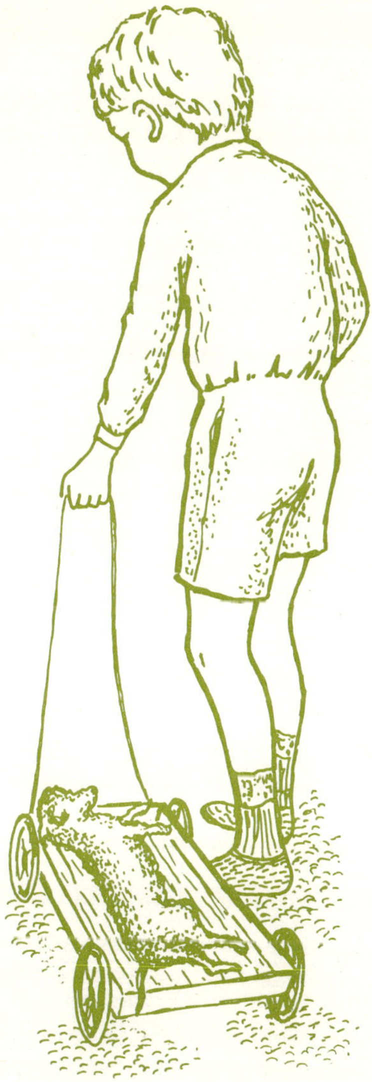

and I'm at a loss. It's too much!' This may seem cruel and disrespectful. It is no doubt self-pitying. But, it is also an intense expression of anger that comes when a person is left alone, feeling helpless and insecure. It isn't abnormal or sinful.

We may be angry at ourselves, berating ourselves for what we said, did, or didn't say, didn't do. There is no way to say and to do all we may ideally wish, for we are not God. Even knowing this does not mean that we don't feel angry.

St Paul encouraged the Ephesians to let their anger out, not to hold it in. 'Be angry, but do not sin; do not let the sun go down on your anger, and give no opportunity to the devil.' Isn't it conceivable that if we really do believe that God is Father, he will be the best of fathers. This kind of Father knows us and allows us the expression of fullest feelings, including our anger. As a loving, understanding Father, he accepts us and our anger without reservation.

Scripture reading
Psalm 4; Ephesians 4:25–27

Why do I want to lash out at you, Lord? I feel guilty blaming you, but I feel so hurt, so angry. I know somehow that you will understand even when I don't understand. You are my Father. Amen.

Going down

'My God, my God, why hast thou forsaken me and art thou so far from saving me, from heeding my groans? O my God, I cry in the day-time but thou dost not answer, in the night I cry but get no respite.' (NEB)

'Why hast thou cast me off, O Lord, why dost thou hide thy face from me?' (NEB)

The Psalms sound out the all-too-familiar cry or whimper of depression. Shakespeare put it another way when he said,

The grief that does not speak
Whispers the o'erfraught heart and bids it break.

The drawn face of Steve, who stood statue-like in his work clothes, gave way to matching words: 'I'm feeling so low. I don't care. I can't get going. What's the use anyway? No one cares or knows what I feel. There's no God of love.'

Depression! It's a sudden or gradual 'going down,' a lowering of emotion that goes much lower than on a usual bad day. With it comes a companion, isolation. Mrs Young said it well: 'I wish to get away. I don't care about anybody. I

wish people would just leave me alone.' This is a frightening feeling for many of us. We don't like to feel down, even though the death of our loved one gives us reason to feel that way. Depression is unpleasant. It has the odour of hopelessness hanging around it. Every cloud does not have a silver lining. In fact, when we're depressed, no cloud has a silver lining.

If someone says, 'You'll just have to get over it. Cheer up a little. Don't worry, you'll be all right,' it may seem cruel. We may want to say something in angry retaliation, but we force a strained smile instead. Behind this is the feeling 'Get away, you don't know. It won't pass!'

When we lose someone close to us, we can expect depression. There is no way to avoid feeling down and out when death takes someone we love. We certainly can't be happy and cheerful! Depression comes like a known but unwelcomed companion to stay for a while. When it does, the dark clouds blot out the sun. Sleep may be difficult. Food doesn't seem important. We may sob quietly. Our memory may seem shifted into neutral. Some fears about what may happen creep in. Depression invades everything we are and we do. It may not completely immobilize us. When it does, especially when this immobilization is prolonged, we need professional help.

Facing the fulness of death is depressing.

Naomi told me that when she realized the impact of death, she felt as if she had fallen into a dark pit. She felt separated from everyone and everything. Nothing mattered. She couldn't pray. Her faith seemed to disappear. As time passed and she attempted to relate to her friends and relatives, to become more active, often at the gentle push and shove of people who really cared for her, she began to feel the clouds of depression slowly move away. As they moved, her faith emerged, as if it had been there, but obscured. She could pray. She could continue her mourning and face her loss. Depression was a sign that she was really facing her loved one's death. It was a signpost to recovery when she began to move through it. Naomi was experiencing not only Jesus's forsakenness on the cross, but also his resurrection power, as she came alive within herself and towards others.

Scripture reading

Psalm 102:1–13; John 14:16–18; Philippians 4:13

Dear God and Father, I feel hopeless and helpless. I feel all light has gone out. Even if I don't reach out to others, let me allow them to reach in to me. I long to experience again that you have not forsaken me. You are faithful and true. Help me to be faithful too. Through Jesus Christ, my risen Lord. Amen.

I'm not feeling well

The psalmist said that we are 'fearfully and wonderfully made.' There is little, if anything, we experience that doesn't affect our total person. When I'm physically exhausted, I have a hard time thinking clearly and quickly. When I'm upset about a relationship, my feelings churn and, as a result, my stomach may ache or my muscles cramp. Our mourning the death of a loved one affects us totally too.

Mr Martin sat slumped across from me and said, 'Since she's gone it hasn't been the same.'

'What do you mean?' I asked.

'Well, she was for one thing a really good cook. Couldn't beat her. Made everything from scratch. Not many women do that nowadays. Yes sir! I guess I got pretty much used to her cooking. I suppose she spoiled me. I just haven't eaten properly since she's gone. In fact, I haven't had much appetite for anything.'

It's not unusual for our grief to give us physical distress. The loss of appetite, loss of weight, and loss of energy, are quite normal. Some of us may react differently, perhaps starting to eat too much. In either case, our bodies feel our personal loss keenly.

One middle-aged widow had headaches though she never had before. Her rheumatism started acting up again. She couldn't understand this until she realized that these physical problems had started shortly after her husband's death. She began to see the connection. Her loss was hard to face, and her body was trying to force her to do it. As she talked, releasing her feelings, the physical symptoms of her grief lessened. She was progressing on her bereavement journey.

If we stop on our journey, physical distress may take over all the more. The physical stresses are built-in reminders to urge us to move on. Those of us who are bereaved in the later years can expect to have more physical ailments. It's as if our ageing bodies felt the impact of our loss more and had less strength to handle it. This doesn't mean we can't. It means the physical distress may be more prolonged and more difficult than that of younger people.

We may experience sleeplessness. In their book, Bernadine Kries and Alice Pattie tell us that 'the nights will be long and tortuous. You will awaken hearing sobs. They will be your own. If you are widowed, you will awaken with an arm outstretched, reaching for the unreachable.' A major loss such as the death of our beloved may cause physical reactions. There can be dizziness, blurred vision, rashes, palpitations, chest pains, shortness of breath, general aching, heavy menstrual periods, fainting, indigestion, and other symptoms.

We can expect much when we are thrust into grief. We can do something too. A physical examination and medication may be appropriate. But the primary thing we can do is to get on with our bereavement journey. As one person put it, 'I was amazed. As I continued to talk, sharing my memories, my feelings, my fears, my hopes, with someone who cared, I sensed my attitude slowly changing. I guess I finally buried my husband. I don't mean physically, but I inwardly "laid him to rest." As I spiritually left the graveyard, having really entrusted him to God, I felt more at ease. I started to look at life again. I began to feel better physically. My medicine helped, but I was able to stop taking it. I really believe it was my changing attitude that helped me physically as well as spiritually.'

Scripture reading
Psalm 142; Matthew 11:28

Grant me the courage to see myself as a whole person in your sight, O Lord. Help me to see your message for me, even when it comes to me through my body. I am your creation: body, mind, and soul. Amen.

I can't go on

A small animal caught in a trap waits for the unknown, frightened about what the next minute may bring. It may have struggled to get free when first caught, but the struggle only tightened the trap's grip. Now there is no more struggle, only hopeless resignation and helplessness.

Helplessness is a feeling we have as we anxiously wait for the report of medical tests. Will it be good news? Will it be bad news? Will it be mixed news? There isn't a thing we can do to change the helplessness of this waiting; nor can we speed up, slow down, or alter its results. As much as we try to remain optimistic, hopeful, and in fair spirits, there is no denying this anxious helplessness.

Losing a beloved person can bring on a similar feeling of helplessness. One person remarked that he could no longer go on living without his spouse. He felt helpless and incapacitated. There seemed to be no reason to live.

Feelings of helplessness are intensified by a

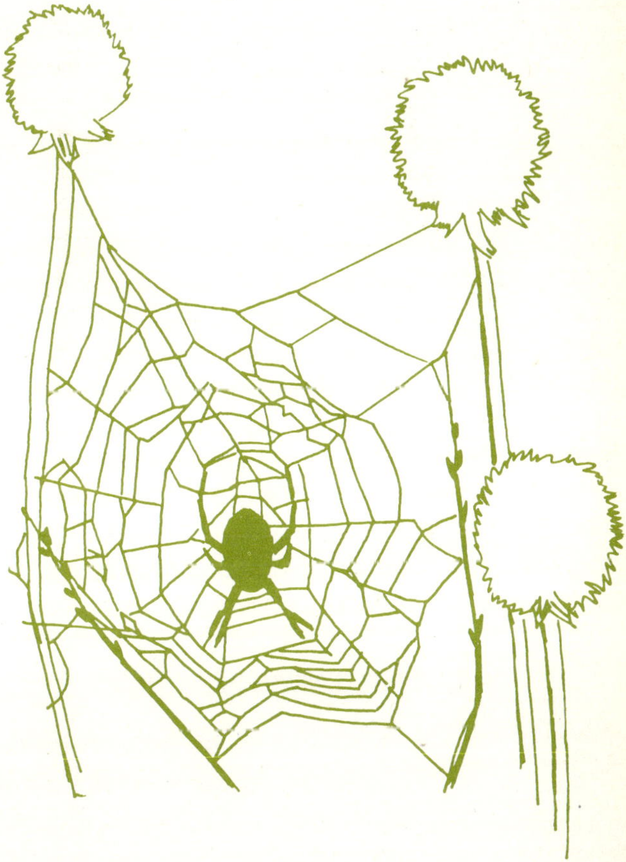

lack of purpose or reason for living. Even though we feel as if we had no choice about our loss, but are helplessly stuck, we have made a choice. Our movement from helplessness to helpfulness largely depends on choices we make, although it doesn't seem that way. We did not choose our loss. But we do choose to let this loss control us if we don't go on living for ourselves, without our loved one. We can tell when this forward movement begins. From 'I can't go on' to 'I won't go on' is a giant step.

When I was a child I was often told, 'there is no such word as *can't*.' What did this mean? I began to realize that this was a backhanded attempt to motivate me. In other words, *can't* is the choice I make when I refuse to do anything. 'No such word as *can't*' was a parental reminder that I have the God-given power to choose otherwise. It is a beautiful moment in our lives when we say, 'I didn't want to go on. In fact, I didn't feel able, but now I want to. I realize I can and I will. I can choose to remain helpless, or I can choose to be helpful to myself.' Then we who have suffered loss through death can say, 'That's what my loved one would want me to do.'

I think of Moses at the beginning of his mission. In answer to God's call to be his leader, Moses said, 'I can't do it.' But the Lord kept knocking down Moses's resistance. The Lord said, 'Go, I will help you.' It took persistence, even emphatic insistence, on the part of God. Moses finally made the move from 'I can't' to 'I won't' to 'I will.' And he did!

God helps us to help ourselves in our helplessness.

Scripture reading

Psalm 86:1–13; Psalm 139:1–18; Romans 5:6

Dear God, it's no fun feeling helplessly stuck, yet I could stay this way and sadly grow to like it. But the world doesn't need another immovable rock. I need a shove to start rolling. I believe I can move if you give me an encouraging nudge. Amen.

Here, but gone

'There was a river separating us. I could look across the river to the other side. I've never seen anything so beautiful in all my life. I can't describe it. It must have been heaven. Then I saw my son looking across the river at me. It was dark and foggy where I stood, but the sun was shining on him. He said to me, "It's all right. I'm OK. Don't worry. I'm happy." Then he turned and walked away into the sun.'

This was one of a series of dreams a mother experienced when she lost her 24-year-old son. No one could talk her out of the reality of these dreams. No one should. This dream, with the others, had significance and meaning. It was the God-given unconscious part of her that was speaking in language plain yet mysterious.

Our dreams and visions may carry great and religious meaning. Dreams are sometimes helpful emissaries, friends to aid our bereavement journey. They speak to reality, to pain, to wishes, to fears, to unfinished and unfulfilled needs, to hope. John Sanford has called the dream 'God's forgotten language.'

The bereaved mother explained what the dream meant to her. She felt that her son was reassuring her, attempting to nurture and to protect her. Prior to his death he was depressed and his life was not going well. This dream place was beautiful. The sun was warm and life was new. He was encouraging her to try harder to let him go.

The friendly dream was helping her to accept her son's death. The fact that she was on the foggy, dark side indicated to her the reality of the dark experience of her loss. She was still in the fog of grief. Not all the work had been completed so that she could stand in the light of her new day. But God was at work.

Many persons have also experienced visions of the dead person standing close to them. Some people have seen the one who died doing something that he would have done when he was alive. It's as if the death never happened. Eventually however, the pleasure of the vision or dream gives way to the sad awakening of the loss through death.

Dreams and visions are important. We can see this in the Bible. Joseph gained position and prestige through his visions, dreams, and interpretations. The visions of Daniel are colourful and intriguing conveyors of messages. Our Lord's birth was announced to Joseph in a dream. In our dreams God may have helpful and meaningful messages of challenge, acceptance, hope, and new birth. We may need help to understand these messages, but we can be sure that we are befriended by God in many and mysterious ways.

Scripture reading

Psalm 3:1–5; Psalm 16; Ephesians 3:14–21; 1 Peter 1:3–9

God, it's only a dream! Or is it? Help me, Lord, to understand what you are saying to me through my dreams. In my journey I need help accepting death and learning to go on living. Amen.

Here and nowhere

Mr Wright put his head in his hands while his body convulsed with sobbing. The crying was painful, choking, burning. He was feeling the wrenching terror of his loneliness.

Mrs Hayes showed me through her home, a small, ordinary house one passes by without looking twice. Why the tour? Mrs Hayes's husband had died, and she wanted me to know what he had been and done. She also wanted to share her loneliness without calling it by that name. She pointed out his carpentry work and tools, the pickles and beans they had canned together, the porchroom he had built, his couch where he had watched TV, their garden. As she spoke, her lips quivered, her eyes glistened, and her body froze for a moment. It was a courageous and painful work of mourning. Her loneliness spilled over in her eyes and her voice as she reminisced.

There is no way to avoid loneliness completely, and it is better not to try, for the very terror of loneliness also contains the sensitivity of being human. Clark Moustakas has said, 'To love is to be lonely . . . All love leads to suffering. If we did not care for others in a deep and fundamental way, we would not experience grief . . . when they are ill and dying.'

Mrs King was a small, thin woman whose husband had died and left her a widow at the age of 50. She was also a deaf-mute. For many days she wouldn't eat much, seemed despondent, and preferred to sleep away time. It took great effort for her to talk through an interpreter about her husband. Once she began using her sign language, her little body, which was curled in a sitting position, began to unravel. It was hard. Laced through this grief of inaudible words were threads and shreds of loneliness. The years they had spent together, sometimes with more bad times than good, still formed a relationship which, when broken by death, created a loneliness never to be totally taken away. Talking about her deep loneliness by talking about her husband and their relationship diminished the hold it had on her. But we knew there was no way to take it all away. One can go on when loneliness is faced, but it remains a shadowy companion.

When we risk facing our loneliness, we may discover new confidence to continue our journey of self-restoration toward meaningful living. By meeting our loneliness we encounter a potential growth experience. No one can do it for us.

Loneliness leaves its calling card in our hearts and on our faces, but it can enhance our dignity and maturity and open new possibilities for tenderness.

One day Mr Sanborn looked at his suffering loneliness and decided he would walk with it. He would be its partner rather than its victim. So he sat down and began to write. He was no writer, he thought, but slowly and falteringly, with words scribbled out and scribbled in, he began to write about his wife and about their life together. His writing, done with his partner, loneliness, at his side, turned out to be a beautiful memoir of his wife and of their life together. He found himself speaking and relating to other people in honest and tender ways. He was rediscovering life, people, and meaning.

Clark Moustakas put it well: 'Let there be loneliness, for where there is loneliness, there is also love, and where there is suffering, there is also joy.'

Scripture reading

Psalm 5:1–3; Matthew 28:18–20; John 16:32–33

Dear Lord and Father, I didn't choose to be lonely. Loneliness came my way and forced itself on me. People don't always understand, but your Son, my Lord Jesus, knew what it was to be lonely. Help me to accept my loneliness so that I may allow it to move me towards people and life. Be my courage and strength, O God. Amen.

Lord, not my child!

I stood beside the stretcher in the hospital emergency ward and looked at the small, lifeless body. For a few seconds my fantasy took over and I saw my own child lying there, motionless. Shock, numbness, fear collided within me. I came to and blocked out my fantasy. The parents arrived and their feelings poured out – screams, tears, shaking. Anger, hurt, agony consumed them. What is it like to shake hands with death's claim on a child?

Death at any age is a shock. But death at an early age? 'Her whole life was ahead of her!' 'Why?' 'It's cruel!' 'Why not me?' 'I can understand an older person dying, but a child?' 'No one really understands.' When we lose a young child to death, life looks as though it has reached its darkest and nastiest moment. Many feelings come and grudgingly leave, if they go at all.

Recovery seems doubly difficult; forgetfulness never completely comes. Hopefully, remembrance can be shaped into living again, without the flesh and blood of a future which will never be. Every child's death is so individual to each of us that the impact can have effect not only on ourselves, but also on our marriage and family. A child's death may claim us like no other death can.

Bill Murray said, 'No one really knows. People try to tell me their concern. Maybe I don't want to hear it. I've been hurting and life has felt terribly unfair. Who can convince me not to feel this way?' Valerie remarked, 'Everything I had hoped for was gone, like that! Those dreams of watching him grow and develop, wondering what he'd become and all those things a mother dreams, wants and fears. Gone!'

Turning the corner of death towards life is agonizing when we lose a child. A scar remains. But, turn we can. Reggie said, 'It took months and months. I admit, whenever I see a child the same age as our Jennifer, I start to re-live our nightmare. In time, though, I've come to weigh life in terms of what we had and experienced with Jenny. She was so young, there wasn't much, but it was good. I can enjoy the little, good memories. You know, I have an entirely different attitude and feeling towards all parents who lose a child. Before, I really wasn't affected. I was sympathetic, but now, I really care! There are many of us – we're not really alone.'

'We're not alone.' That says a lot. One person

has described baptism as God's hugging a child. In turning the corner from death to life, perhaps we can one day affirm that our child really is eternally hugged by God, in spite of death, through death.

Scripture reading
Matthew 18:1–6, 10; Mark 10:13–16

O God, I can't believe that you took a child from me because you love and need my child more than me. Help me not to confuse people's ideas with your intentions. I need to know, again, that we are yours, from the beginning. Help me to know you have my child in your eternal love. Please soothe my wound with your grace. Amen.

You'll never know

St Augustine said, 'All this grief, my heart was utterly darkened . . . I was miserable and without joy.' Pain and despair are threads that run through us as we move through our journey of bereavement. How many times have we said or heard, 'The dead have it made. At least they have peace, but I'm left with the suffering. Sometimes I feel I'd rather be dead than alive. At least I'd not have to face all this!'

In pain and despair we can echo the words of the old spiritual, 'Nobody knows the trouble I've seen. Nobody knows my sorrow.' We may have been moving through our journey slowly, doing well, when suddenly the reality of our loss, this death, hits again! There is no going back, no recapturing or retrieving what was lost. Our loved one is gone. The pain invades and grips, and the fulness we were beginning to feel seeps out. Emptiness takes over. The wound opens wide and we despair. It's as if all life stops again.

Mr and Mrs Johnson had spent 64 years together as man and wife. 64 years! That in itself seems like a lifetime! Just before their 64th wedding anniversary Mrs Johnson was taken to the hospital with what seemed to be a bout with one of those unnamed viruses. Mr Johnson remained at her bedside. One afternoon, in the course of normal nursing care, the nurse asked him to step out of the room. Moments later, when he came back, he met not life but death. His wife had quickly and quietly died.

Mr Johnson's life had been bound up with his wife. The more we have our lives bound up with one another, the more vulnerable we become. So it was with Mr Johnson. The shock, disbelief, and guilt over having been so close – a few steps away – and yet so far apart, eventually gave way to painful despair. His beloved wife had silently been cut out of his life by death.

One doesn't have to be married 64 years to feel the pain and despair of death. It is not time, but our closeness to our loved one that increases our vulnerability and opens us to deeper pain and despair. Yet when we confront our pain and despair and begin to accept the loss, surrendering ourselves to God in our powerlessness, then pain and despair can give way to hope. The unwanted pain can be accepted and transformed. When we accept our pain as our own, suffering can grow into compassion. It's as if the heart opens, and out of sorrow come warmth and joy.

The life and death of each of us has influence on others: 'If we live, we live for the Lord; and if we die, we die for the Lord. Whether therefore we live or die, we belong to the Lord.' (Romans 14:8 NEB).

Scripture reading
Psalm 31; Luke 22:39–44

Dear Father, time and again I feel the grip of despair and the pangs of pain. My loss is hard to bear and accept. I wonder how I can go on. I pray, and I'm not sure that you hear. My despair gets the better of me. I remember Jesus's despair on the cross. You heard your Son in that dark moment. Even when I doubt, you do hear me. Help me, Father. Amen.

I know

You talk about your problem with a friend, who says, 'Yes, I know what you mean.' Yet the feeling you get is that this person *doesn't* know.

We, too, may have let these words spill out of our mouth. We may have been trying hard to understand another person and wanted that person to know that we were feeling with him.

But there really is no way to know another person's experience of loss and grief. Each of us is unique, and our experience is truly our own. Yet some people come close to knowing our bereavement experience. They somehow convey that they really walk with us in our loss. Perhaps they have experienced a loss like ours. It helps if this person is one who is sensitive and knows what we may be going through, but doesn't use our grief as an occasion to talk solely about his own grief and bereavement.

When we lose someone we love, we are uncertain. We may really wonder whether anyone knows what our loss feels like and means to us. Some people are able to turn our doubtfulness into the certainty that someone does know. At that point we feel assured and buoyed.

I recall a man who lost a young son in a tragic accident. Before the funeral people came to give their sympathy, concern, and support. This father had the feeling that most of the people were indeed being kind and concerned in a most uncomfortable and unsettling situation. They didn't really know what to say except the usual clichés and the expected sympathetic talk. He felt their uncomfortableness and their sincerity, but the words were common and cold.

During this difficult time, one man came into the room, went to the coffin, and walked towards the bereaved father. He said nothing. He simply looked into the father's eyes for a few moments, touched him on the shoulder, and left. Not one word was spoken, but a well of wordless messages had flowed.

Later the bereaved father said, 'There were many kind people, but they didn't know what to say. I know from all the people who came that they cared. But there was one person who really spoke to me. He didn't say anything. He didn't have to. I knew by his look and his manner that he knew what I was experiencing.' This person, too, had lost a child through death.

That was an 'I know' meeting of two hearts. It brought assurance. Words aren't always necessary when the heart knows. Doubt is turned into certainty, and this brings comfort in the middle of pain.

Scripture reading
Matthew 5:3–12; John 10:11–15

Dear God, I have moments when I'm not sure anyone knows what I'm going through. I want to believe someone knows. What I need even more is to realize that you know. Help me to think about your Son, O God. If I think about Jesus, I'll believe that you do know me in my pain. Amen.

A swinging pendulum

I once took a ferry boat to Martha's Vineyard off the Massachusetts coast. Though it was a large secure boat, I found myself moving up and down, leaning first to one side, then to the other. There was no way to feel still and stable, centred. No matter what I did, I was controlled by the rising and falling of sea waves and by the boat's listing.

After the death of her husband, Wilma felt like a clock's pendulum. Her emotions moved from one side to the other. She felt wound up, and her feelings were in constant motion. She said, 'There seems to be at least two of everything in me. I feel caught between opposites. I feel the loss of Bert and it hurts me. Then I feel relieved he's gone. If he had had to be laid up, inactive and suffering, he wouldn't have liked it. I'm not sure I could have taken it either. So sometimes I wish he were here, and then I'm relieved he's not.'

She went on, 'Some days I remember the good times and a few of the not-so-good times we had together. Other days I want to forget and can't. Then I think, maybe I ought to sell the place and move; my son says I can come and stay with him. But I look at the place and say, "No, I'll just stay here." That's not all! There are times when I want Bert to depend on. I don't like having to do everything he used to do. Before you knew it though, I learned how to do the things he used to do, and I even like some of that responsibility. In fact, my independence lets me do as I will.

'I'm probably going to get a job like I wanted. When Bert was alive, he didn't want me to work. You see, one minute I want to be dependent and the next minute I like my independence.'

Wilma was experiencing some of the opposites of bereavement.

Unsettling as this might be, it indicates movement in the bereavement journey. Out of these tensions comes energy which helps us to accept our loss and embrace our future. Coming to terms with the opposites we experience within us helps us find ourselves. If we lean only one way, we may be impeding our bereavement journey. Opposites together make something whole.

There is no day without night, no resurrection without death. As we move between our opposites, we can pray the words of an old hymn:

Jesus, Saviour, pilot me
Over life's tempestuous sea;
Unknown waves before me roll,
Hiding rock and treacherous shoal;
Chart and compass come from thee,
Jesus, Saviour, pilot me.

Scripture reading
Matthew 7:7–8; Romans 8:28; Philippians 2:12–13

Move with me and in me, O God. As I work towards being myself and coming to a new wholeness in life without my loved one, be my compass and guide, through Jesus Christ, my Lord. Amen.

Much ado

Most of us want help when we lose a loved one. But what kind of help, and when?

At the time of death there may have been people who wanted to do everything for us. They may have insisted on calling the relatives and starting funeral arrangements. At home they may have made the coffee, prepared the meals, and helped beyond what was helpful. You may have been one of the number of people who, in spite of appreciation for this help, felt it was too much. As difficult as it was and as grief-laden as you may have been, perhaps you felt you could have handled more of the work yourself.

Or maybe you did most of the work yourself. If you did, you were probably coping with the initial shock of your grief.

As time passes, what do we find ourselves doing? How busy and active ought we to be? Tennyson, after the death of his friend Arthur Hallam, wrote: 'I must lose myself in action lest I wither in despair.'

When the Huffmans' son died they moved

back and forth between activity and inactivity. There were days when they couldn't concentrate on the smallest task. Mrs Huffman would begin to write a letter and never finish it. Household work was started and stopped. Sometimes it wasn't even started, but was left neglected. Dust gathered, rugs looked tracked, dishes piled up. Sheets went unchanged, flowers even went unwatered. There seemed to be no energy for anything. Then everything was reversed for a time. The Huffmans felt an overwhelming burst of energy. Activity reached almost a frenzied pitch. Work, work, work! Go, go, go! It was as if they were busy trying to forget. Then their bodies gave way to exhaustion and sleep, but they awakened to the memory of their son's death. It may be that the extremes of all activity or no activity were temporary roadblocks on the bereavement journey.

King David was rebuked by Joab, his commander-in-chief, when David found out that his son, Absalom, was dead. David had gone to his room weeping. Joab reprimanded David and told him to get on with it. Their troops had been victorious. The king, David, and the court were alive. To mourn on a day of victory was shameful. David was to bury his grief, since the people's good came before personal sorrow. This was good military ethics, but doubtful guidance in helping David mourn satisfactorily. David was not the same again. To be forgetful too soon may be an unhelpful denial.

Some of us may feel that we have to get busy. Perhaps well-intentioned people say to us, 'Take a trip, visit the relatives, change jobs.' We may even think we should sell the house with its well of memories and move away.

Travel may be helpful when we're ready for it, but when it comes to irreversible decisions like moving and selling, it is better to mull it over before we act. We need to work patiently and wait to make decisions. Our impulsive desire to change things may be a momentary need to escape our loss and suffering. We need patience and time to plan helpful and purposeful activity.

Scripture reading
Isaiah 40:28–31; Colossians 1:9–14

Dear God, give me patience and a sense of what helpful activity is for me. Show me when I need to slow down. I don't want to block my journey, but to move onward. Make me aware of your presence in my movement. Amen.

Yes

There are many landmarks in our bereavement journey. *Acceptance* is certainly one. In fact, much of our mourning is working towards acceptance. Some of our mourning follows the acceptance of our loved one's death. We begin to reaffirm ourselves in our acceptance of our loss. We may recall how hard it was for the disciples to accept Jesus's prediction of his death. We may also recall the discovery, acceptance, and affirmation of the centurion who stood at the cross and declared, 'Truly this man was the Son of God!'

Moving towards acceptance isn't easy. There are days when we feel we have accepted this death, our loss: 'Yes, this has happened. It is true.' Other days we hedge: 'I know it has happened, but it seems too unreal. My head says one thing and my heart feels something else.'

Mr Bernard said to me following the loss of his wife, 'I know she is dead. I must go on without her.' The symbol of his finally accepting the loss of his young wife was the gravestone he purchased and placed as his last gift to her. Once he had done that he could inwardly leave the cemetery. His act represented final acceptance of her death.

We live with the acknowledgment that death is in life, without giving it much thought until it hits our lives. If we dwelled on death, we would probably not be living well. But when it hits, we are faced with it. It is no longer the other person, but me! I have lost! We may think we have accepted it, but the disharmony within us and our outer lives and relationships says we really haven't fully accepted it.

I sometimes view older people who seem to go on as being invulnerable. But when a man I knew died unexpectedly, I couldn't and wouldn't believe it. I had built the illusion that he would go on for ever. The fantasies we build make acceptance a slow process.

Mary had accepted her dying and was ready. Jack, her husband, was working at it. Towards the end Mary said goodbye to her husband and family, kissing them and admonishing them to love and care for one another. It was a heart-tearing and beautiful moment. She closed her eyes and slept. Hours later she woke to find she hadn't died and gone to heaven. When she saw all of us she realized death was still eluding her. She was angry. She wanted to die. She had accepted her death. There was no chance for survival. Her body had not reached the point of death, even though her emotions and spirit had reached it. Four days later she died.

Later Jack said, 'I too had pretty much accepted Mary's death. But when she survived after we had said goodbye, I found myself thrown back. The four days were more of what seemed like unnecessary suffering.' The interruption indicated how tentative and fragile the initial step of acceptance is.

There is no easy way to accept death. We each must find our own process. We may be helped by good memories, by time, and by expressing our feelings. When our acceptance is coupled with self-affirmation, we have made a great stride. Arlene put her affirmation this way. 'John wanted me to go on. As I work to lead my own life without him, I'm really accepting what he gave me, the freedom to be me.' What a gift of acceptance!

Scripture reading

Matthew 26:36–42; John 20:24–30

As Jesus commended his spirit to you, O God, help me to see that my acceptance of this death is the doorway to new life. As death led to resurrection, so lead me to experience the acceptance that brings newness to life. My security is in you, my Father, through Jesus Christ. Amen.

Through a glass darkly

'You know, it's a funny thing.' The old gentleman looked pensive. 'I don't mean funny in the humorous sense, but it's a strange thing. I think for my Alice quite often. Her death was hard, and I took it hard. I knew it was coming, but death was like a stranger – a stranger you don't really know, even though he's always around.' This man was struggling with an unresolvable issue – the mystery of death. Even if death is seen as a result of man's fall in sin, it is still a mystery.

In the Old Testament it is death that the man of faith sees as a threat to his relationship with God. It was life that was to be felt and experienced in relationship with God. The stranger, death, was the mysterious visitor that could bring this meaningful, covenanted relationship with God to an end.

Jesus did little preaching or teaching about death. He didn't see death as a roadblock to our relationship with God. Jesus emphasized life and its fulfilment. His own death was overcome by his victorious resurrection. Jesus didn't say much about what happened to people after they died, but he promised everlasting life to all who believed in him.

Paul saw death as the enemy, but an enemy defeated by Christ. Death is our foe, but 'Thanks be to God who gives us the victory through our Lord Jesus Christ.' We take heart and hope in this resurrection victory.

Marlene Browne said, 'For a long time after my mother and then my husband died I experienced not only bitterness but fear. I was fearful of death, life, the future. Death seemed to squeeze the life out of me. I felt like an empty shell.' Marlene fought back, wrestling herself out of this stranglehold of death. The first indication of victory appeared when she became aware that death, the stranger, would be her enemy only if she allowed it to be. She didn't need to be controlled by it. Why? She realized that she was worshipping life for its own sake. The more she worshipped life and her lost relationships, the more death took over.

Then she remembered Mary's encounter with Jesus in the garden. Marlene substituted her name for Mary's and heard Jesus saying, 'Woman, why are you weeping?' Then, in her mind, she heard him say, 'Marlene!' She began to make the turn from defeat to victory. Death the mystery, became death the door to hope. It was another beginning.

Scripture reading

John 12:44–50; Romans 11:33–36; 1 Corinthians 15:51–58

Dear Father, my death and the deaths of people I love are a mystery. Although I may not give up searching out the mystery, I do want not to torture myself to know the unknowable. You have penetrated and conquered it. My hope is in you; I need no more. Your saving grace is enough. Thank you, through Christ my Lord. Amen.

There is a season

The author of Ecclesiastes wrote that 'there is a season for everything, a time for every occupation under heaven: A time for giving birth, a time for dying.' Does that mean that beyond the natural rhythm of life which we see in the change of seasons there is also a rhythm and reason for what occurs? Is there a purpose in the death we've experienced?

To one man, death was no more than the end of life. Death itself meant nothing. Anything purposeful was contained in the life lived. Death was the sword that declared 'the end.'

On the other hand, there was the woman who said, 'Having to face the fact that my husband was dying made us value our love for each other with an intensity and intimacy we had not known before. Every day became a gift to experience together. No longer did we take life or our relationship for granted.'

Marge said, 'For a long time I couldn't accept the death of my son. I cursed God for snatching this precious life from me! As I let go of my anger and directed my attention to my two remaining children, I made a discovery. My relationship to my children and my husband began to grow in a way I hadn't experienced before. My husband and I went through an agonizing period that nearly ended in divorce. But we worked at our feelings and relationship with the help of others. Out of the ashes of our loss and conflict came a new life, a new commitment to our marriage.' They moved out from themselves towards mutual involvement in church and charity work, particularly with other parents who had experienced the death of a child. They grew in personal maturity, marital fidelity, and intimacy. Was this caused by their child's death? They would say that since their tragic loss, their lives had taken on new meaning and value.

In Christ, life is intended to have purpose. Perhaps we all too easily become worshippers of life. We may make life itself into an idol. If all our marbles are in a basket called *life*, death may indeed be the unwanted, purposeless intruder. This is not to say we shouldn't 'have life and have it more abundantly,' as Jesus said. But to make anything, including life, into the 'be all and end all,' squeezes God out of the picture. It is our relationship with God in life that enables us to make sense out of seeming nonsense. Even when sense and purpose seem to escape us, we trust that one day we will

understand. On that day we will come face to face with the author of life.

A courageous statement was made by a person who, in struggling to understand the death of his beloved, said, 'I still do not see the purpose. I struggle, but I don't give up. Somehow I feel that in my very struggle with this I am choosing to say that there is purpose and meaning.' Giving up may mean the quiet desperation of despair. There is wisdom in the search and struggle.

When Jesus met Martha, she said to him, 'If you had been here, my brother would not have died.' Jesus answered, 'I am the resurrection and the life; he who believes in me, though he die, yet shall he live, and whoever lives and believes in me shall never die.' Do you believe this?

Scripture reading
Lamentations 3:31–33; Philippians 3:12–16

Lord, I do believe. Accept my times of doubt and feelings of purposelessness. Help me understand your purpose for my life. Guide me in my search for personal truth. Hear my prayer, O Lord. Amen.

Those old feelings

'Sometimes I felt guilty for even feeling my own sexual desires. I suppose I tried not to think of sex, you know what I mean . . . I felt maybe it was un-Christian. I guess I just didn't think about my sexual life for a while. I don't think I wanted to. I was preoccupied with other concerns and with my wife's memory. I felt it might be almost violating my love for my wife. She died almost ten months ago. I don't feel that as much as I did a few months back.'

Some Christians are able to discuss sexuality freely and openly. Others feel that to talk about sex borders on the sinful, yet our sexuality is a real and God-given part of us.

Most literature on grief doesn't mention this natural aspect of our lives, but it is good for us to deal with our sexuality as part of our bereavement journey. How can we simply ignore something that has been a vital part of our relationship? When a loved one dies, the relationship to that person, who lives on in us, is as real as if it still existed. If this person was your marriage partner, grief has dulled temporarily the sexual feelings and desires. As these feelings and desires emerge quite naturally from our underground of grief, we have choices to make. It isn't sinful or wrong to have these desires. We aren't being unfaithful to the deceased loved one, even though we may feel as if we were.

There are those who choose to and can live quite contentedly without sex or marriage after the death of a loved one. Others may find that sexual desires return after the grief wears off.

God calls us to fulness after our loved one dies, just as he did before the death. Since our sexuality is as individual as our fingerprints, it is more important for some than for others. The point is that in our bereavement journey the rediscovery of sexuality is good. It can be a sign that we are risking making headway towards embracing ourselves, others, and life.

Scripture reading

Genesis 1:26–28; Genesis 2:23–25; 1 John 4:13–19

Lord, it sometimes isn't easy to think about my sexuality, let alone to talk to you about it. I'm not ashamed of being human, but I get uneasy admitting personal and intimate thoughts and feelings. Yet you are my Father. Help me to trust you. In trusting your understanding of me, O God, I can better trust myself. Amen.

Reaching and touching

'Death ends a life,' said Robert Anderson, 'but it does not end a relationship, which struggles in the survivor's mind towards some resolution, which it never finds.' None of us can really erase a meaningful, loving relationship when death closes the door on it. We may not see it, but we know it is there, inside of us; we know it is a part of us.

One man expressed what many feel: 'It has been three and a half months since Marguerite died. I've had many dreams in which she seems to be alive, but morning comes and I am alone in bed. It's been helpful to have so many warm feelings flood over me. I've seen people with whom Marguerite was especially close. I am still seeing people and places through Marguerite's eyes. I remember her soft warmth and I also remember her anger about all the forces in the world which encourage hate, mistrust, and greed, preventing people from living as human beings. I can look back on the past three years and know that our relationship grew and deepened so that these years became the most

meaningful of our nearly 28 years together.'

Moving forward in our bereavement towards new relationships does not mean the end of the remembered relationship. The old relationship is not meant to hold us back for ever, but to help us in engaging in new relationships.

Making this transition differs for each individual. For some of us, old friends may want us to return and to relate to them as we did prior to the death. This can be unfair and unrealistic. It is better for us if we move into relationships that have real meaning and satisfaction for us. These may include our old friends, but may not, in truth, include all of them. One woman told me, 'Some of my friends are well meaning, I suppose, but sometimes I wish they would go away and leave me alone. They want me to act like nothing's happened!'

Nancy related 'I let my friends know when I was ready to rejoin them in our flower club. They were a little pushy at first, but I made it clear, "When I'm ready, you'll know!"' Nancy had her mourning and her relationships well in hand.

One of the most unsettling prospects may be that of establishing a close relationship to a person of the opposite sex. A real platonic friendship is a possibility and a good solution. It is especially good for those of us who have always enjoyed the opposite sex while still maintaining a personal Christian ethic that makes sex without marriage wrong. A companionship relationship can be a stimulating and fulfilling blessing. This works when we want to share time with the other person without the deep, responsible emotional involvement which love in marriage brings.

Mrs Michaelson said she had always enjoyed the companionship of her late husband's men friends. In fact, she said, 'My husband was the kind of man who was glad I could enjoy the company of his friends. They knew our relationship wasn't sexual, but simply good and interesting friendship.' Mrs Michaelson continued, 'I now occasionally see a few of these men.' They continued the meaningfulness of their relationships. No marriage was intended just platonic friendship. This may not be usual for most of us. Yet it can be a valuable help in the process of affirming ourselves and other people.

If you contemplate and struggle with the possibility of remarriage, you may find the words of Joseph C. Landrud helpful: 'The way out of this seeming impasse is to return in meditation to the *memory* of our love relationship with the departed. Was that love relationship truly free, spontaneous, self-giving, and life-affirming? If so, it is no healthy testimony to the quality of our love for someone to say that when he or she died our ability to love also died. Authentic love which, in its deepest form, is the love of God expressed through us to all, without limit and without end, could certainly find a new object in the world around us. It is this deep and limitless love that truly makes us free.'

Whether we contemplate remarriage or not, it is important to embrace some people in relationships which give meaning and vitality. Our bereavement journey is not one of separation, but one which steadily moves towards people.

Scripture reading

Matthew 22:35–39; 1 John 4:7–11

Dear God, give me courage to reach within and to reach out. Lessen my fear to touch the lives of others. Enable me to receive and to give, like Jesus, your Son and my Lord. Amen.

Constant care

'At first you did not love enough; And afterwards you loved too much.' These lines from Stephen Spender may express the deeply felt but seldom spoken refrain haunting those of us who feel we loved too much. 'If we hadn't loved each other so much, hadn't been so close, maybe I wouldn't hurt so now. I can't let go and I can't go on.'

This love of ours has lost its intended receiver. Although there is no longer responding love, the memories of our relationship and of our love together remain with us, etched permanently into our being. We keep these etchings even as we journey forward. Edith Sitwell has said, 'Love is not changed by death and nothing is lost and all in the end is harvest.'

A pastor in Wisconsin whose wife died from cancer expressed some of his 'love etchings' this way. 'We believed in God, but realized that our faith did not guarantee us any special treatment or length of days. The quiet touch of hands as we watched a sunset over Lake Mendota, or the eager excitement as we watched thousands of

geese come into Horicon Marsh, or a quiet dinner with friends, each took on a special depth of meaning which was felt, but hard to realize.'

A mother who had lost her son said that her love for him would never die. 'All my love wasn't wrapped only in my son. He will be with me as part of me, but my love will not be limited; it never has been.' Her love knew no rigid perimeters. It was flowing out to touch others. In this love she reached beyond death into life.

The floods of mourning cannot drown the force of love that reaches beyond the grave. Love lives beyond death, into resurrection. Love cares, reaches out, gives, feeds. It goes beyond the self and even beyond our loved one. Nothing, not even death itself, can ultimately separate us from the love in Christ Jesus our Lord. Death has been conquered. Love is freed to flow.

Scripture reading
John 14:15–21; 1 John 4:7–12

May my memories be a living love. May my loving be more than a memory. O God, grant me the assurance that death has lost its sting in the victorious love of my resurrected Lord. In that name of Jesus Christ, I pray. Amen.

Springs in the desert

The desert wanderer moves on in the hope that he will find an oasis with water and shade to sustain and fortify his life. There may be periods of parchedness in our bereavement journey when we, too, long for a spring in the desert – times of dryness that seem to push us towards hopelessness. To give hope to the discouraged people of his time, Isaiah used that same image of a spring in describing the blessing that was to come through God's Saviour. Included in his hope-giving description was the vision of 'water gushing in the desert, streams in the wasteland, the scorched earth becoming a lake, and the parched land springs of water.'

Having a future that reaches beyond the death of our loved one requires hope. Hope belongs to life and reaches beyond death. According to the Bible we don't create hope, but receive it from God.

Jim Meyer said, 'While my son was dying, I and my wife searched frantically and hopefully for a cure. We never lost the hope that something would be discovered that would yet save our son. After he died we still kept aware of any developments that might have helped our son but that now would be of help to other people dying from cancer.' He continued, 'This hope is important. When I realized that the chances of my son being the recipient of a new cure were becoming fewer and fewer, I became more realistic about it, but the glimmer of hope was always there.' Hope was sustaining to him and his wife.

After the death, hope took on another dimension. It now became a matter of having a future. It became a matter of meaningful survival, a survival that would expand into fulfilling and meaningful relationships. Jim described his hope as coming to him as a gift. 'I played a part. I had to struggle, but I felt God was at work creating it in me through my bereavement struggle. I found myself reviewing and renewing my relationship to my other three children. I began to see that the future I needed to embrace centred around the meaningfulness of my life with my wife and family. I had really neglected them.'

The loss of his loved one actually pushed him towards those he loved. The dryness of his loss led to springs of rebirth in his surviving relationships. He went on to say, 'Perhaps hope reached beyond death into life and relationships in this way.'

There was one more way. Jim's hope was for now and for the future. His hope was in Jesus Christ, who would one day come to reunite and make new. In Christ was the eternal hope that became a vital part of Jim's thoughts of his future in life and in death. Isaac Watts put it this way:

O God, our help in ages past,
Our hope for years to come;
Be thou our guide while life shall last,
And our eternal home.

Scripture reading
Romans 8:22–25; 1 Thessalonians 4:13–18

Hope springs eternal even when I'm unaware. As water gushes beneath the surface, unseen, your gift of hope is there for me. Help me to tap it for new life. In it is the Spirit, pointing to my eternal home where my loved one also dwells. Amen.

The prized possession

In the letter to the Philippians, Paul says, 'For I have learned, in whatever state I am, to be content.' Paul wasn't talking about grief or the mourning process, but what he says is significant for our bereavement. 'Whatever state I am in' could apply to all the life crises you and I experience, certainly including the death of our loved one. 'I have learned . . . to be content' indicates that the contentment of peace doesn't always just happen, or come to us suddenly without our working at it.

Some people may have experienced a peace that seemed to fill them unexpectedly. A man told me about the death of his father: 'I drove to the small country church where my father's funeral service was held. I sensed the quietness of the countryside, the beauty of the woods I passed, the warmth of that summer day. I felt a dawning peace break within me. In a matter of seconds I felt this peace come all over me. I knew that God was with me.' The man was at peace with death and the loss of his father.

For many of us peace is something that grows

gradually within us. With Paul we learn to become content with our loss. A young couple lost their eight-year-old daughter, who died from leukemia. In their bereavement process they reached a point of acceptance which brought them peace. They put it this way: 'We have come to the conclusion that we regret nothing with Anne. At first we regretted all the years we wouldn't have with her, all the years she wouldn't have to grow and experience life and become a woman with a life and future. She didn't have that and we didn't have that with her. But we've experienced to the full those eight years we had together. No, eight years for Anne and for us were a lifetime. We're thankful for eight years and we're learning to be at peace.'

This couple did something that may be hard yet instructive for us. They began to measure life not by the number of years, as we and society easily do, but by the quality of life each of us is privileged to have. They realized that it isn't how many years we have as much as what we are and do within those years that is important. In making this major movement in attitude they found peace.

The peace which some of us may come to is simply the inner knowledge that, 'Yes, my loved one and I are safe in Jesus's keeping.'

Words always fall short of expressing exactly

the inner certainty and comfort of peace. We acknowledge this when we say, 'The peace of God which passes all understanding, keep your hearts and minds through Christ Jesus.'

Scripture reading

Psalm 23; Isaiah 26:3; Matthew 11:28–30

Encourage us, O Lord, to find peace in the full realization of our loss. Strengthen us in the faith that peace isn't an elusive dream, but a heartfelt reality that comes after a hard-fought journey. As Jesus came to peace with the words, 'It is finished,' help us to come to the point in our pilgrimage when we too can say, 'It is completed.' Amen.

A mustard seed

'If only I had more faith, I'd feel better. I'd be able to handle myself in this situation.' How much faith is enough in our mourning? Some of us feel that it is always more than we have. Jesus said that the amount of faith isn't important: 'For truly, I say to you, if you have faith as a grain of mustard seed, you will say to this mountain, "Move hence to yonder place," and it will move; and nothing will be impossible to you.'

A grain of mustard seed! Do you recall how small a mustard seed is? Necklaces used to be worn with a mustard seed in the bulb, which magnified it so that it could be seen with normal eyesight. Now if we have faith, though it be that small, nothing will be impossible.

I interpret faith in this instance as basic trust. We don't need a huge quantity of it in order to get on with our bereavement. In fact, if we worry about having a lot of faith, we may miss the mustard seed we do have.

Our mustard-seed faith will help us move the mountain of grief. Peggy said, 'I have often become discouraged trying to work through my grief. I still feel like giving up sometimes. I wonder if I'm going to make it, and ask, "How long is this going to take?" Then something in me says, "Peggy, you can do it. Don't give up." I feel some kind of trust, and I keep going. That little spark gives me confidence to try. I have life ahead of me, even though it's not the same.'

Peggy was, in her own way, talking about her experience with the mustard-seed faith.

The giver of this grain of faith is God, whose Son, though despondent and despairing in his crisis, maintained his faith. He went through his Gethsemane of grief with the word 'Father' still on his lips.

We too can go through the valleys and mountains of our bereavement journey with 'Father' on our lips. Our hearts may wonder, doubt, and cry out in pain, but these feelings will not obliterate our faith. Even when we think we have lost that mustard seed, we do well to remember that our Father is faithful.

Scripture reading

Matthew 9:20–22; Romans 5:1–5; 2 Corinthians 5:1–8

O God, help me to trust in and through the shadows of my grief. A small seed can do so much. It can split the mountains of my grief and create new life. Amen.

The community of faith

'Here was a group of people who understood my grief. They listened. They cared. This has been one of the biggest helps to me. It has helped me to live, to reach out of myself to other people. I finally began to crawl out of my protective shell. I didn't find it easy to share my loss. I was ready to give up. I felt no one could ever have gone through what I was going through. But this group of fellow suffering, caring people reached me. I stopped feeling sorry for myself, and I found I could be helpful to some of them. I have really regained faith in myself, my friends, my God, and my church.' These are the words of a person involved in a church grief group.

This small group of people met regularly to share their losses with one another. Our bereavement journey is not easily travelled. A group of travellers who share human losses can make the journey a supportive and integrative experience. The church is not only a place in which to thank and praise, but also to share sorrow.

I remember singing an old hymn, 'My

church, my church, my dear old church.' For some of us the church hasn't always been dear. The birth of helping groups, such as grief groups, may rekindle some of the dearness of the gathered community of faith. Perhaps you don't have a group like this in your church. You may be able to start one. No one is a stranger to loss. We are people who experience death and losses within the church community. We aren't alone.

The church, as a community of the faithful, has been at the work of grief, bereavement, binding the brokenhearted, for a long time. The church has been about this before any formal grief group was ever organized. We and people through the centuries have gathered to share confession, absolution, song, prayer, Word and Sacrament, the risen Christ. Gathering to reflect and praise, we come with our grief to have it understood by a grieving Lord who triumphed over the grief of death. Here we experience the Shared Sufferer who can rekindle our faith and help us to come through our darkest hours.

The community of faith stands to touch continually our innermost bereaved self with collective support and the offer of renewed life through the goodness in Jesus Christ, our Lord and Saviour.

Scripture reading

Ephesians 2:19–22; 1 Peter 2:9–10

The church's one foundation is Jesus Christ, her Lord. Help me to lean on this rock that will not crumble, but will support me through grief to life. Amen.

What lies beyond?

Speculation and controversy surround our ideas of what happens after death. There is a great interest in what lies beyond the grave.

What I share with you comes from the lives of people who, like us, experienced the death of a loved one and tried to face the absence. They confronted the abyss of death and asked, 'What now?' I will not forget the elderly lady who had lived her life wanting to experience everything possible. She had that unusual attitude which led her to risk experiences. She said to me, 'I don't want them to stick needles in me, tube me, and do all sorts of things to numb me, push me into unconsciousness, and then keep me alive, without me knowing it.' She was firm and angry. 'I don't want any of that stuff. I want to experience my own death!'

I asked her, 'What then?'

She said, 'I've always tried to experience things. I won't be cheated out of experiencing my own death. Then, I don't worry. I'll be in the hands of God and that's enough for me.'

Wilbur told me that he didn't think about the

afterlife very much these days. He felt he would one day see his wife. For him it was enough to know that she had believed and said to him, prior to her death, 'I'll be in heaven.'

Maggie said she believed her loved one had been reclaimed by his Father, who was her Father, too. 'I feel the pain and loss, but I know he's home.'

A. J. Gossip's wife died. This Scottish minister had had a companionship with his wife that had been evident to his congregation. When he returned to the pulpit for the first time after his wife's death, his sermon title was, 'When life tumbles in, what then?' The closing lines of his sermon on crossing the river of grief would not be forgotten by those who heard him. 'I, too, like Hopeful, can call back to you when one day in turn you will have to cross it, "Be of good cheer my brothers, for I feel the bottom, and it is sound." '

Search, think, feel, look, ponder, try. Yet, let us take our ultimate assurance in this, 'Let not your hearts be troubled; believe in God, believe also in me. In my Father's house are many rooms; if it were not so, would I have told you that I go to prepare a place for you? And when I go and prepare a place for you, I will come again and will take you to myself, that where I am you may be also.' A room prepared for my loved one, and for me.

Scripture reading
Psalm 91; John 14:1–11

My restlessness and my wondering are sometimes satisfying. Sometimes they get the better of me. Regardless of my continual search for the tomorrow beyond, lead me to find my rest in you, O God, my eternal Lord. Amen.

Amazing grace

In Jesus Christ we come closest to seeing and knowing the grace of God. Grace, to use one theologian's definition, is 'to accept the fact that I'm accepted even though unacceptable.' This tries to get at the sheer, total giving of God. It is the undeserved, yet freely given gift of acceptance of us by God in Jesus Christ. This reaches beyond all we say, do, and go through.

Harvey and Faye said, 'As we made our bereavement journey we kept getting the idea that we *had* to go through all the expected feelings and stages. Not only that, we felt we had to go through our mourning well. In other words, it had to be good mourning, not done poorly! We felt constrained to end our journey affirming life, all put back together. For our mourning to be good, we had to be successful at it!' But here's where the word of grace came into their lives. They said, 'It dawned on us that we didn't have to mourn scientifically or necessarily be successful. God's grace in Jesus Christ meant that even if we weren't able to make our bereavement journey a success, even if

we never reached the end, even if we found ourselves in despair, grace embraced us.' They were saying that they were accepted in their mourning, even if they were unacceptable and unsuccessful in working it all through.

Amazing grace! How sweet the sound
That saved a wretch like me!
I once was lost, but now am found,
Was blind, but now I see.
The Lord has promised good to me,
His word my hope secures;
He will my shield and portion be
As long as life endures.

We thank God that he doesn't stand aloof above us, but is involved with his creation. He has redeemed life and death in Christ. Our very bereavement journey is a journey surrounded by and immersed in grace. Thank God!

Let us receive the benediction of grace to our bereavement journey:

The Lord bless you and keep you. The Lord make his face shine upon you and be gracious unto you, in your going out and in your coming in, in your rising and in your lying down, in your mourning and in your peace, in your labour and in your leisure, in your laughter and in your tears, until you too come to stand before him in the day to which there is no sunset and no dawn. In the name of the Father, and of the Son, and of the Holy Spirit. Amen.